Affiliate Marketing

Establish Your Passive Income Stream By Following A Meticulous Guide For Generating Online Revenue, Which Will Bolster Your Digital Presence

(Strategies For Establishing A Profitable Affiliate Marketing Enterprise)

Maurice Broadbent

TABLE OF CONTENT

Commence Your Affiliate Marketing Journey Now. 1

Select An Appropriate Marketing Strategy. 9

Your Product 46

The Originator And Trailblazer Of Affiliate Marketing 65

Establishing A Customer Base And Promoting Your Merchandise 93

Commence Your Affiliate Marketing Journey Now.

To embark upon your voyage as an affiliate marketer and commence generating income through online channels. I will thoroughly guide you through all the necessary information and actions required to become a proficient affiliate marketer in the present day.

Choose the Appropriate Niche: Aspiring affiliate marketers should consistently make well-informed decisions when it comes to selecting products for promotion on their affiliate website or blog, contingent upon their dedicated expertise. Additionally, it is important to consider that you have the freedom to discontinue the sale of a particular product if it is not performing well, and select an alternative product of your preference.

Select the Appropriate Affiliate Program: this necessitates conducting extensive research on companies that offer a lucrative affiliate program. It is imperative that you ensure the selected product possesses high quality standards that align with your market segment.

Devise an Effective Strategy: As an affiliate marketer, it is imperative to meticulously plan and establish the most fitting strategy. This includes defining your target market, gaining comprehensive insights into your customers' interests and demographics. This will facilitate the generation of engaging topics and discussions that will capture their interest, thus effectively increasing traffic to your website. Furthermore, endeavor to apply ingenuity when arranging your affiliate link so as to captivate individuals' interest and incite their curiosity.

Listed below are three prevalent challenges encountered by individuals involved in affiliate marketing:

Selecting an erroneous affiliate program: Numerous individuals aspire to swiftly generate income through the realm of affiliate marketing. Amidst their eagerness to conform, they often gravitate towards popular products as part of the prevailing trend. These are the types of products that they perceive as being "trendy" or popular. They select the product based purely on its market demand, with little regard for personal appeal or preference. This decision appears to lack prudence and foresight. Rather than succumbing to popular trends, endeavor to select a product that genuinely captures your interest. To achieve success in any undertaking, it is imperative to allocate sufficient time for meticulous planning and strategizing one's actions.

Please select a product that captivates your interest. Subsequently, conduct a comprehensive investigation into the market demand for the said product. It is inherently easier to market a product for which you possess a genuine passion, as opposed to one driven solely by monetary gains.

Participating in an excessive number of affiliate programs: Given the straightforward process of enrolling in affiliate programs, there exists a potential temptation to engage in multiple programs concurrently, with the aim of optimizing one's potential earnings. Moreover, one might perceive a lack of issues and potential drawbacks in actively participating in multiple affiliate programs.

Indeed, that strategy offers the potential for diversification of income streams. Nevertheless, partaking in numerous programs and endeavoring to advocate for all of them simultaneously would impede your ability to focus on each individual program.

The result? The full potential of your affiliate program remains untapped, and the anticipated income may not align precisely with your initial expectations. The most effective approach to achieving optimal outcomes is to participate in a singular program that offers a commission rate of no less than 40%. Subsequently, exert maximum dedication by displaying fervent enthusiasm in promoting your products. Once the profitability of the venture becomes apparent, you may consider enrolling in another affiliate program.

The methodology involves executing it gradually, yet relentlessly. There is truly no necessity to hasten the process, particularly in the context of affiliate marketing. Given the current trajectory, it appears that the future holds promise and indicates a sustained presence of affiliate marketing over an extended period.

Abstaining from purchasing the product or availing oneself of the service: As an affiliate, your primary objective entails proficiently and persuasively endorsing a product or service, while actively seeking out customers. In order for you to accomplish this objective, it is imperative that you effectively convey to the clientele the specific product and service. Hence, it presents a challenge for you to undertake these actions when you yourself have not personally tested them. As a result, your ability to effectively endorse and advocate for them will be inadequate, thereby hindering their chances of promotion. Additionally, you will be unsuccessful in generating a sense of inclination among your clientele towards engaging with any of the products or services you have on offer.

It is advised to engage in a personal trial of the product or service before committing as an affiliate, in order to ascertain its fidelity in delivering on the proclaimed benefits. If such is indeed the case, you are among the esteemed individuals who possess firsthand knowledge of both the merits and demerits inherent in the matter. Your clientele will subsequently perceive the authenticity and genuineness emanating from your demeanor, inducing them to personally experience your offerings.

Numerous affiliate marketers are committing these errors and facing severe consequences as a result of their actions. In order to prevent oneself from encountering a similar predicament, it is highly advisable to take every possible measure to steer clear of repeating past errors.

Time is the key. Dedicate a moment to evaluate your marketing strategy and ascertain if it aligns with your objectives. If executed with precision, you can optimize your affiliate marketing program and achieve elevated levels of profitability.

Select An Appropriate Marketing Strategy.

The Foremost Consideration in Marketing
Build your audience.
Whichever strategy you opt to implement for your affiliate marketing enterprise must center on cultivating your target audience.
Why?
The existence and prosperity of your business heavily relies on your audience. Lacking a customer base that appreciates and fervently supports your offerings, your endeavors would be rendered fruitless.
It is important to bear in mind that one of the primary objectives of affiliate marketing is to generate profits and establish your enterprise to eventually facilitate the launch of your own product.

Through the endorsement of affiliate offers that align with the forthcoming product's niche, you are cultivating an audience comprising individuals who possess a genuine interest in the upcoming offerings. You will engage in various strategies to promote products, while simultaneously prioritizing the continuous development of your email database.

Possessing an email list grants you a significant advantage.

In the event that you opt for the utilization of Google Ads as a promotional strategy and achieve satisfactory results, you might be inclined to underestimate the significance of cultivating an email list, which serves as a valuable asset of your audience. However, what transpires when Google places a ban on your account for violating a rule of which you were unaware? It happens. A lot.

Relying on other platforms for sustained business growth can leave you vulnerable to potential failure in the event that your account is suddenly terminated, resulting in a total disconnect from your audience and potential downfall.

Renowned TikTok affiliate marketer, Jonathan Montoya, boasted an impressive following of 190,000 individuals on his account. He shared a video that TikTok deemed to have violated the community guidelines, resulting in the suspension of his account. Although this setback greatly hinders his progress on the platform, his business continues to thrive as he strategically accumulated a substantial email list through the provision of complimentary guides and training, thus garnering individuals' email addresses.

Will this have a negative impact on his business in the immediate future? Absolutely. He severed his connection with his primary audience. Will it significantly impact his business? Absolutely not. He displayed intellectual acuity and successfully constructed his roster of email contacts. Additionally, he possesses the expertise required to amass a substantial TikTok following, consequently ensuring a swift recovery to his desired position. Moreover, armed with previous experience, he has now acquired the knowledge to avoid the actions that led to his previous ban, thus ensuring he will not face another instance of being barred.

If you have a desire to observe his advancements in reclaiming followers and wish to adhere to his account, kindly visit tiktok.com/@jonathanmontoyalive, or alternatively, explore the name 'jonathanmontoyalive' within the application itself.

Establish and expand your email subscriber base by incorporating effective marketing techniques across various channels. The key lies in establishing a loyal audience.

Your Approach to Marketing

Having selected your affiliate programs and determined their suitability for your new affiliate business, it is now imperative to devise an effective marketing strategy to promote those products and disseminate your links to the target audience.

It has been established that we should refrain from indiscriminately distributing our links and instead keep our primary focus on assisting individuals in resolving their issues. In order to accomplish this task effectively, it is imperative that we devise a comprehensive strategy to locate individuals who are in need of our assistance.

There exist three primary approaches through which individuals can be reached. You have the capability to create videos, generate written content, or disseminate audio materials.

Video

In terms of video, there is a slight learning curve involved. You require a certain type of instrumentality in order to effectively disseminate your message to your intended audience. This could potentially involve utilizing your mobile device to engage with individuals on popular platforms like TikTok, or alternatively, leveraging the landscape mode of your smartphone to effectively communicate with individuals on YouTube.

Additionally, it is imperative to consider the timing for video production when devising a content plan which revolves around video.

You require a suitable location in which to capture videos of superior quality.

Perceptions of quality can vary depending on individual perspectives. It is essential for the video quality to be free from graininess and any resemblance to a recording made on a vintage camcorder discovered within your grandmother's attic. The significance of your message supersedes all else; nevertheless, its appearance must not resemble trivial content, as this may hinder its receptivity.

As a busy parent myself, I understand the challenges of finding a suitable environment with sufficient tranquility for recording high-quality audio for videos, particularly when there are boisterous children at home. Kindly bear this in mind should you contemplate embarking on video production.

I have encountered numerous instances where the children engage in quiet activities in an adjacent room, leading me to mistakenly believe that I can discreetly capture a brief video for platforms such as TikTok or YouTube Shorts. One can infer the subsequent events. During the brief 60-second interval, my children, in a playful manner, opt to forcefully enter the room, engaging in imaginative roleplay of Luigi's Mansion (a video game I introduced to them, resulting in their intense fascination), and expressing loud vocalizations concerning King Boo.

Perhaps not the most commonly cited illustration, yet it conveys my intended meaning. It is imperative that you carefully allocate a dedicated area and undisturbed periods to facilitate video production. Therefore, it is incumbent upon you to determine at this moment whether you are able to make this requisite commitment.

There are mobile applications available that enable video editing, and they offer user-friendly interfaces and affordable pricing. I possess a video editing tool which I acquired for a cost of $15 and employed it for the purpose of editing my TikTok videos. I possess a mobile device running on the Android operating system and make use of the YouCut Pro application. Applications such as TikTok, YouTube, and Facebook all offer various editing capabilities embedded in their platforms for short-form videos. Thus, if you are inclined towards creating shorter videos, you may readily find cost-free solutions to commence your endeavors.

As previously stated, there is no requirement for us to adopt a Hollywood approach; you have the option to commence with your smartphone and subsequently upgrade to a professional video camera as financial resources become available for reinvestment in your enterprise.

Writing Text

In the realm of written content, there exist multiple approaches to marketing through textual means. We shall now proceed to discuss some of them in the forthcoming sections.

Blogging

The most obvious method of writing for affiliate marketing is that you can start a blog. There is a prevailing belief among many individuals that blogging has become obsolete, but I personally hold a different perspective on the matter. In contemporary society, there is a general lack of interest in mundane details such as one's breakfast choices, which significantly diverges from the original purpose and essence of blogs. Individuals engaging in discussions regarding their personal experiences.

However, it is frequently observed that when individuals conduct online searches in order to obtain solutions, blogs often appear in the search engine results pages (SERPs) displaying the sought-after information. Crafting blog posts not only enhances the discoverability of your website but also serves as an invaluable means of assisting individuals by providing answers to their inquiries.

If individuals are conducting a targeted search query aimed at resolving their issue and your blog appears in the search results, it presents a significant opportunity. When they read your post and encounter a satisfactory response and rudimentary solution within the article, there is an increased likelihood that they will proceed to click on your affiliate offer or willingly subscribe to your mailing list by means of your opt-in feature.

Acquiring a high ranking on Google necessitates a significant amount of time investment, particularly when contrasted with expedited approaches such as YouTube and TikTok. In order to be deemed worthy of ranking by Google, it is typically necessary to possess a well-established and high-quality website. It is not invariably true, however, the factor of time undeniably works in your favor when it comes to SEO (Search Engine Optimization);

essentially, the practice of enhancing your online visibility.

This constitutes my primary means of promotion as I enjoy the process of constructing my website, and it proves challenging to produce video or podcast content amidst the presence of active children. Additionally, I derive great pleasure from constructing a personal asset that will generate dividends indefinitely. An esteemed video channel with a large subscriber base is also quite commendable, yet one must exercise caution since platforms have the capability to abruptly terminate one's account. By transferring your files to a different web host, it is possible to promptly resume your operations with a website, all while preserving your esteemed Google rankings if the transition is executed swiftly and accurately.

Social Media
There exist methods through which you can integrate social media into your blogging strategy with the purpose of

disseminating your content. One favorable aspect of utilizing social media is that once you create an article, there is no need to await its ranking by Google. If one were to create a podcast or video, it would be possible to disseminate it among their social media followers in order to obtain initial viewership. You may disseminate that piece of content to your social media audience or commence expanding your social media presence through the content you are sharing.

If you possess the capability to compose articles and generate a substantial audience through social media platforms, it is indeed a valuable asset. This is because it brings forth unpaid traffic to your website. You can be discovered through user-initiated searches, as well as appearing in their News Feed or For You section. Individuals engage with your content and subsequently, a portion of them proceed to interact with your promotional material within the article. A specific percentage of these individuals may convert into customers if the promotional content is strategically positioned. Consequently, there is no necessity to allocate financial resources for generating traffic.

However, as previously mentioned, achieving a high ranking in search results can be a lengthy process. Therefore, it is necessary to consider alternative methods of promoting your content in the interim. I will further elaborate on this matter in the subsequent chapter, where I will discuss my meticulously designed content marketing strategy that effectively disseminates my content to the target audience, without having to rely solely on Google's judgment of suitability.

Similar to how it is advisable to concentrate on a single affiliate offer initially, it is equally important to commit to one platform that you seek to excel in. Identify the platform where your target audience congregates and devote valuable efforts towards creating and sharing substantial, beneficial content.

I am aware that many experts strongly advocate for the establishment of a Facebook group centered around the topics in which you aim to promote affiliate offers. If your objective is to advance educational initiatives tailored to children, you might consider adopting a name such as Educational Programs for Children or Educating Today's Youth, or a similar designation that aligns with your cause.

Subsequently, by generating informative content that addresses users' needs, you are effectively contributing to the affiliate marketing process. It is crucial to refrain from indiscriminately sharing your links across the group in order to maintain a positive user experience. Individuals may choose to depart from the collective if they perceive that their experience primarily comprises sales pitches without adequate delivery of utility or benefit.

The utilization of Facebook groups in conjunction with a well-devised blogging strategy would prove advantageous, as it enables the opportunity to inquire whether individuals would be interested in perusing your most recent article, thereby aiding them in finding a resolution to an issue they are commonly confronted with. And subsequently, you have the ability to share the hyperlink with individuals who already possess a genuine interest in the subject matter you are discussing. Social media can play a significant role in your strategic marketing plan, aiding in the dissemination and promotion of your multimedia content, including videos, written text, and audio materials. Please ensure that you maintain singular concentration on a single platform at a given time, until such time as you have successfully established your devoted audience.

Writing a Book
Written material may also take the format of a literary publication. If you aspire to create a publication and engage in self-publishing through Amazon, this represents a viable avenue whereby you

can effectively extend your reach to a wider audience.

You have the option to incorporate hyperlinks to your own supplementary website, where additional resources and free materials are made available to individuals seeking further solutions to their problems. Subsequently, within the framework of that website, it is possible to incorporate affiliate offers.

To compose a book, one must possess a certain level of expertise or accomplishments in the subject matter, without which credibility and reliance on one's insights may be undermined. It is essential for you to demonstrate that you have achieved the goals they aspire to achieve, in order for them to recognize you as the individual capable of guiding them from their current position, where you yourself used to be, to their desired outcome, which aligns with your present state.

It is important to consider that if you are at the nascent stage of your career, embarking on writing a book may not necessarily align with your immediate objectives. To successfully accomplish that, it is essential to possess a substantial level of expertise and proficiency. This diverges from a blog or video in which you have the ability to initiate the education of individuals regarding the knowledge you acquired, regardless of when you initially acquired it.

Are you interested in obtaining a noteworthy exemplar of a book that features a supplementary website containing advantageous affiliate links? You're reading it.

Audio

Finally, I would like to address the topic of audio. Sound can serve as an excellent medium to engage an audience. The predominant manifestation of this phenomenon in contemporary times is the practice of podcasting.

An approach to disseminate a podcast involves producing an audio recording and supplementing it with a stationary visual graphic, subsequently uploading it onto the YouTube platform. Although this approach may be suitable for individuals with stringent financial constraints, it is advisable to seek out a podcast host capable of handling the distribution of your content on your behalf.

I employ the bCast platform to facilitate the distribution of my podcast. A proficient podcast host will not just undertake the responsibility of hosting your episodes, but also furnish you with the necessary resources to conveniently enlist your podcast in the numerous podcast directories available. When a host is connected to directories, each episode published is automatically disseminated across multiple platforms. It offers an incredible dissemination to a diverse array of destinations without any additional exertion required.

The primary purpose of the podcast is to provide assistance to individuals with their superficial challenges, conduct interviews with industry specialists relevant to the endeavors one aims to promote, and ultimately establish oneself as an authority figure in the field being promoted. It's kind of like a blog, but in audio form.

Furthermore, it is important to refrain from overtly imposing your offer on others. Rather, the aim is to establish a connection between your offering and the subject matter being discussed in the episode.

Within my podcast, I extensively discuss topics such as sales funnels, business strategies, motivation, and the cultivation of unwavering focus. I possess the capacity to engage in discussions encompassing diverse subjects while simultaneously establishing connections to various products and services I endorse through affiliate marketing.

If you are interested in observing the manner in which I engage in podcasting, I cordially invite you to explore the episodes available at mastersalesfunnels.com/podcast.

BuzzSprout also serves as an effective platform for hosting podcasts. I have created podcasts for a different organization using the renowned platform BuzzSprout, which is considered one of the leading players in the podcast hosting industry due to its established reputation and prominence.

In the event that you opt for podcasting, it is imperative to ensure that you possess a well-curated list of topics, so as to avoid depletion of content for recording and dissemination among your audience. While this holds true in the case of video and blog production, as individuals anticipate a regular release schedule, it is worth noting that the direct downloading of videos and blogs onto mobile devices is not a common practice for most people. However, it is noteworthy that applications such as YouTube have the capability to alert subscribers when a new video is uploaded, and push notifications have emerged for blogs as well.

Podcasts are actively subscribed to by individuals, and the latest podcast episodes will be automatically downloaded to the user's device. Consequently, if you happen to skip a week, your audience will begin to experience a sense of absence. There is a possibility that they will terminate their subscription, or alternatively, they may opt to transition to a competing podcast in search of the desired information and entertainment.

Ensure that you diligently prepare a comprehensive content list in advance to avoid any instances of writer's block or last-minute cancellations of the show.

I would like to offer a suggestion: I would caution against placing undue reliance on a podcast format that necessitates securing a new guest each week, as obtaining suitable guests on a consistent basis can pose a challenge. You should not be discouraged by this, as including guests in the equation enhances the overall interest. Additionally, you will benefit from the advantage of having your guest disseminate the podcast among their own followers. They also aspire to gain significance, and appearing as a interviewee on a podcast serves as a commendation on their professed expertise. They will engage their audience by introducing your brand to a new demographic. That's how growth happens.

If you are able to identify individuals with affiliations that are complementary to your business in the field of affiliate marketing, then you can effectively broaden your reach by gaining exposure to a new and interconnected audience.

This brief overview provides an overview of the diverse content strategies available for promoting your affiliate offers.

I shall provide a more comprehensive analysis of each of these aspects during the discussion on my employed marketing plan and elucidate methods for creating a customized content marketing plan in a subsequent chapter.

Utilizing Camtasia Video to Enhance Click-through Rates

Given the increasing number of individuals engaging in affiliate marketing, it is unsurprising that the level of competition is intensifying. The examination involves striving to surpass diverse affiliates and exploring methods of achieving this objective.

Furthermore, a comprehensive range of advice and strategies are being imparted to these affiliates, intended to optimize their approach to the program in order to maximize their earnings.

What could be a more effective approach to impress your prospects and clientele than documenting and disseminating high-quality, dynamic, and online screen-captured videos? It is greatly rewarding to witness the fruits of your diligent efforts when your clients eagerly anticipate purchasing your product in such close proximity.

This is the live embodiment of Camtasia. It is an established fact; providing your clients with visually engaging content has the potential to significantly boost your online sales without delay.

There is no requisite for undergoing preparatory stages or formal education in order to possess the capacity to comprehend the mechanics of this framework and its efficacy for your affiliate program. Anyone has the capacity to create astounding recordings, utilizing instructional exercises and step-by-step presentations readily accessible on the internet. The process bears a resemblance to the scenario of having one's clients in close proximity, observing one's desk, while one presents to them the visual and auditory information they desire. This is accomplished incrementally.

For those who are unfamiliar with it, what is the operational mechanism of Camtasia?

1. It has the ability to effectively consolidate your workspace activities into a single action. Do not expend effort on the preservation and arrangement of

each and every one of your documents, as they are stored conveniently nearby and subsequently.

2. Can easily convert your videos into web pages. Once the conversion is complete, your clients will be able to visit that particular page. Audio recordings are more conspicuous and distinct in contrast to the process of reading texts, which typically poses a laborious endeavor.

3. Transfer your pages. Disseminate them via online journals, syndicated content feeds, and webcasts. You may argue that your Camtasia recordings should circulate and reach out to potential clients in the future. Contrary to the widespread visibility across various platforms and websites for self-promotion and conveying your message.

There are various tasks that can be performed using your affiliate program through Camtasia. You can…

Create compelling interactive media introductions that have been proven to enhance sales through active engagement of all senses. Moreover, this also serves to alleviate hesitancy among discerning customers.

Mitigate the impact of discounts and address client concerns by outwardly demonstrating the proper usage of your product and providing effective implementation guidance. Protests will similarly be constrained as the actual elements and the exhibition exist solely for the customers to observe and acquire knowledge about.

Promote affiliate products and services through visual presentations. This approach offers a convincing strategy for redirecting your viewers seamlessly to your affiliate site upon completion of the video. Maximize the opportunities provided by the exhibition by strategically positioning your booth and enticing visitors to access your site directly, offering them comprehensive information and resources.

Considerably augment the potential of your online sales by effectively communicating the value proposition you have to offer to your audience. According to the reports, the integration of visuals in bartering transactions leads to a quadruple increase in the rate of sales. Imagine the considerable increase in elevation if we were to consider them as recordings.

Disperse critical informational products with the potential for selling at significantly elevated prices. It will prove to be a worthwhile investment considering the richly colored designs, menu options, and templates that you will employ.

Minimize the occurrence of miscommunication with your clients. Presenting the necessary elements of your affiliate program promptly enables recipients to clearly perceive its underlying content. One advantageous aspect of media is that there is a limited potential for negative outcomes. It currently exists at its present location.

These are just a subset of the capabilities that Camtasia offers, all of which possess notable utility within your chosen affiliate program.

Please be aware that the primary purpose of utilizing Camtasia is to enhance the revenue generated from your affiliate program. Although it may be utilized for leisure and enjoyment purposes, which is not a particularly valid justification for why you choose to provide assistance throughout that difficulty.

Strive to focus on the goal you have committed to achieving, and achieve it by utilizing resources that can significantly contribute to increasing your earnings.

Boost Commissions Overnight

In the realm of affiliate marketing, it is not a prerequisite to possess one's own website, administer clients, administer discounts, engage in product promotion, or offer support. This is one of the most effortless methods for venturing into e-commerce and gaining additional profits.

Having acknowledged your current enrollment in the affiliate program, what subsequent action might be required of you? Could we potentially increase your bonuses by twofold, or perhaps even triple the amount? What approach would you take to accomplish that task?

Here are some effective strategies to expedite the disbursement of affiliate program payments.

Acquire knowledge of the most effective program and items for progress.

Undoubtedly, it would be essential for you to implement a strategy that will enable you to maximize the outcomes within the shortest feasible timeframe.

There are several factors to consider when selecting such a program. Select the options that possess a commission structure that is conducive to a liberal framework. Offer a selection of items that align with your preferred interest group. Furthermore, it should be noted that the company has a notable track record of efficiently and punctually compensating their affiliates. Should you encounter difficulties in constructing your projects, it may be prudent to discard the current program and persist in seeking more suitable alternatives.

There exist a plethora of online affiliate programs that serve as a source of incentive for individuals to exercise discernment. It may be necessary for you to make the optimal selection in order to mitigate the risk of losing your advertising funds.

Create complimentary reports or concise digital publications to disseminate from your website. It is highly probable that you are competing with other affiliates who are promoting the same program. If you embark on the creation of a concise report that is centered on the promotion of the product, you will effectively distinguish yourself from the rest of the affiliate marketers.

In the reports, provide pertinent information to liberate. If possible, kindly provide some recommendations regarding the items. Digital books offer a heightened sense of credibility. Customers will perceive this quality in you and will be enticed to assess the merits of your offering.

Collect and retain the email addresses of individuals who have chosen to avail themselves of your complimentary digital books.

It's undeniably true that individuals don't make a buy on the primary requesting. It may be necessary to communicate your message repeatedly in order to successfully negotiate an agreement.

This serves as the fundamental rationale behind the necessity of collecting the contact information of individuals who have downloaded your reports and ebooks. You can schedule future appointments using these contacts as a means of reminding them to make a purchase from you.

Acquire the contact information of a potential customer before directing them to the seller's website. Please be aware that you are not promoting or endorsing the item owners in any way. You receive reimbursement solely upon the successful conclusion of a transaction. If you were to direct prospects directly to the merchants, it is likely that they would be permanently lost to you.

Nevertheless, once you acquire their names, you can consistently transmit additional marketing communications to them in order to establish the opportunity for a recurring commission rather than a solitary transaction, if you will.

Disseminate an online brochure or electronic magazine. It is always preferable to recommend a product to an acquaintance rather than offering it to a stranger. This serves as the rationale for the dissemination of your own pamphlet. This also enables you to cultivate a relationship based on trust with your subscribers.

This approach involves skillful integration of informative content with promotional elements. If you consistently produce informative publications, you will be able to establish a sense of communication among your readers, potentially prompting them to support your business by making purchases.

Kindly seek an augmented commission from the dealers.

Should you achieve success in a particular promotion, it is advisable to approach the merchant and engage in negotiations regarding a commission rate for your sales.

Should the dealer possess exceptional abilities, it is highly probable that they will accede to your request rather than risk the loss of a valuable asset in yourself. Please bear in mind that you are seen as a highly reliable investment by your shipper; therefore, do not hesitate to suggest the possibility of receiving a bonus for your outstanding performance. Make a concerted effort to employ a rational approach to the matter.

Craft robust pay-per-click advertisements. The method of employing a PPC web crawler proves to be the most effective approach for online advertising. In your position as an affiliate, you have the opportunity to generate a modest income through the management of pay-per-click campaigns such as Google AdWords and Suggestion. Thus, you should endeavor to conduct an evaluation to distinguish the more effective advertisements and those that should be eliminated.

Assess these systems and observe the significant impact they can have on your bonus remuneration within a concise timeframe.

Your Product

Methods for Choosing a Product or Service?

Now that you have expressed your interest in pursuing a career as an affiliate marketer, the subsequent course of action entails carefully determining the selection of products you wish to endorse. The choice of the product or service you opt to endorse will ultimately determine your achievement as an affiliate marketer. "When endeavoring to choose a particular product, it is imperative to ponder upon the following inquiries:

Does the product to which you are presently inclined possess a polished aesthetic, reliable client feedback, and an effectively constructed sales platform? What would be the optimal target market for marketing this particular product? Is this product within a specialized market which aligns with your level of comfort? In the following segment, you will acquire knowledge on various procedures that can be undertaken to meticulously choose an optimal product or service for promotion in the role of an affiliate marketer.

Compile an inventory

Prior to selecting a product to promote as an affiliate, it is imperative to create a comprehensive inventory of products that pique your interest. Based on the niche you have selected, you could generate an extensive inventory of products that pique your interest. The subsequent course of action entails refining the previously created list by eliminating any products that will not contribute to obtaining a respectable commission. What is the methodology by which this action is achievable? It is necessary to explore various affiliate programs corresponding to the products that pique your interest. Examine the commission that will be accrued for each of those products. If you have concerns regarding the relatively low commission associated with the product, it is advisable to promptly remove it from your inventory. Opt for products that yield a minimum revenue of $30 per sale.

Target market segment

The subsequent aspect that necessitates consideration prior to choosing a product to be affiliated with is identifying the market niche associated with said product. The market can be appropriately partitioned into 23 principal categories. Therefore, it is essential for you to meticulously browse through the various categories and choose a product that aligns with your preferences and that you feel confident in endorsing. When choosing a product to promote as an affiliate marketer, it is essential to prioritize sorting the results based on its market gravity. The magnitude of a product's influence is directly correlated with its level of sales. Therefore, any product exhibiting a greater level of gravity will consequently observe an elevated rate of sales. It is imperative that the market gravity of a product remains at 20 or below. One may be inclined to choose a product with a market gravity exceeding 100. If a product demonstrates significant market appeal, it will inevitably entail encountering formidable competition. For individuals who are new to this subject matter, it would be prudent to refrain from utilizing such products. In the event that you choose to select a product that faces intense competition, it is imperative to devise exceptional tactics for the promotion and marketing of said product. The key to achieving success in the face of intense competition lies solely in the implementation of an exceptionally effective marketing strategy.

Market

Another aspect that should be taken into account prior to choosing a product to promote as an affiliate is the demand and necessity for that particular product. You have the potential to generate significant commission through affiliate sales if you select a product that effectively addresses customers' needs or urgent problems. It is imperative that there exists a robust and sustainable demand for the product within the market. In the event that you are able to locate a product that satisfies this particular requirement, you may proceed to initiate a freeze on that choice. If you possess a product that you believe aligns well with affiliate marketing, you may opt to choose it. As an example, it would not be prudent to engage in the promotion of ice skating products when one is aware that the winter season is nearing its conclusion. Conversely, if you are aware of the approach of Christmas, it can be anticipated that numerous families will engage in culinary activities during the holiday season, thereby enabling you to deliberate upon a food-related product.

Generate revenue through affiliate marketing

Engaging in affiliate marketing presents itself as one of the most straightforward methods to generate income through online platforms. There is no obligation for you to engage in activities pertaining to the generation of product ideas, the process of product creation, the provision of customer support, or any other challenges that may arise in connection with the conception and development of a product. Your sole requirement is to engage in the promotion of a product.

Prioritize the Increase of Website Traffic and Practice Patience

Affiliate marketing prospers through the engagement of individuals who are inclined to click on links to appealing products. However, the question arises as to the identity of these individuals. All individuals who access your blog or website with the intention of perusing the content you have authored. Therefore, it is crucial that your blog or website exudes utmost appeal if the objective is to attract their attention. Please be reminded that in order to secure an affiliate marketing opportunity, it is important to build a substantial and engaged readership. The content on your blog or website should possess a level of engagement that mirrors its visual appeal.

If your website fails to attract a substantial number of distinct visitors, the likelihood of achieving click-throughs to your affiliate is diminished. In this context, the term "unique" pertains to prospective customers who have not previously engaged with your brand, as opposed to your loyal customer base who may have already bookmarked your website and visit frequently. The website or blog's traffic experiences growth as the volume of visitors rises. Not all individuals will be inclined to click on the provided links, therefore, in order to garner a substantial number of clicks, it is imperative to have a considerable number of consistent visitors. In addition, it is imperative to establish a solid reputation as an authority in your particular field in order to gain the trust and confidence of others, thereby enabling them to be more receptive to your recommendations. There should be engaging and compelling content that captivates readers and keeps their attention. It would be inconducive if they were to make a singular visit and promptly disregard your blog. It is imperative to carefully monitor and document the volume of individuals accessing your webpage on a daily, monthly, and annual basis. This will enable you to gauge the true popularity of your blog.

A singular quality product or business suffices.

Now that we have comprehended the individuals responsible for ensuring the influx of favorable traffic, let us examine the areas that will capture their attention.

Inexperienced individuals entering the system frequently commit the error of inundating their webpage(s) with a multitude of diverse elements, under the assumption that consumers are more likely to make purchases when presented with a wide range of options. It is customary for individuals to desire a wide range of options in various aspects, including the presence of numerous links on a website. As you are not a retail establishment, it is not essential for you to provide an extensive range of options to your customers, given that their intention upon accessing your website may not necessarily be oriented towards making a purchase. Their purpose is to provide information, and should you possess a commendable aptitude in your endeavors, you shall have the ability to convincingly compel their purchase whilst they are present, thus affording you the opportunity to amass financial gains.

Consider it an elegant opportunity to exclusively promote a single website, one that caters to the utmost satisfaction of your readers. In other words, you will be afforded the opportunity to effectively market and promote a single product or service instead of having to allocate resources towards promoting multiple ones simultaneously. In addition to potentially causing confusion among your customers, it will also result in confusion for yourself. You are required to thoroughly assess two or three distinct corporations and deliberate on the most fitting placement for their affiliations. Envision yourself as a specialized promotional outlet exclusively showcasing a single product, rather than a diversified marketplace with an array of options.

The principle of persuasion is effective on a majority of the clientele. They are more likely to develop a favorable disposition towards something, provided that you inform them of your offering a product that you have personally examined and approved of.

Do not commit the error of overwhelming the audience with an excessive array of choices at once. If you have listed a single product on your website, offering it at the most competitive price in the market, then even if visitors momentarily leave your site to conduct a brief price comparison, they are highly likely to return specifically to your site and click on the advertisement. Additionally, directing your attention towards a singular product or business simplifies the process of optimizing keywords to be more effective in driving desired outcomes. Therefore, it is advisable to maintain focus on a single business venture or product. If you desire to further expand your efforts, it is advisable to establish separate websites for each affiliate, with a primary focus on individual management rather than allocating resources inefficiently. Subsequently, you can establish connections between your websites.

Significance of Content

This holds true for all websites, naturally, but it assumes even greater significance if your goal is to generate income through affiliate marketing. Individuals visit websites with the intention of seeking both knowledge and amusement concurrently. Thus, it is imperative to ensure an ample amount of content is developed with a strategic focus on the products or business that are being promoted.

It should be noted that search engines possess the capability to assess the presence of high-quality content on a website, leading to a proportionately higher ranking. This implies an increase in visitor count and, ideally, a corresponding boost in sales. You are expected to possess a comprehensive understanding of the concept of "SEO". SEO, an acronym for search engine optimization, pertains to the practice of optimizing websites for improved visibility and ranking on search engine result pages. You are likely aware that numerous companies possess commendable SEO teams that aid in their ascent to prominence. Indeed, this statement holds true as these teams will diligently engage in the advancement of the company's websites and blogs, ultimately enhancing its visibility on the upper echelons of Google search rankings.

It is necessary for you to select all the key terms from your blog or website that are highly probable to be typed by individuals. If they successfully match the combination of words, your website will be displayed as the highest-ranking links. In addition, you may employ a concise explanation to incorporate all the key terms.

However, it is important to note that solely relying on a well-crafted SEO description will not suffice; you must also ensure the presence of high-quality content. Therefore, refrain from employing keyword-focused promotional language when generating content for your blog. Instead, strive to educate, inform, and entertain your audience without engaging in spamming practices. Long articles are not necessary. In fact, posts consisting of 300 words will captivate your audience more effectively than a single post containing 800 to 900 words. The larger the amount of information you provide, the more substantial the audience will be. The majority of individuals tend to seek out websites that provide a comprehensive exploration of complex subjects. By simplifying the process for them, you will have an opportunity to expand your audience.

It is imperative for you to strive for maximum differentiation and individuality. For example, should you desire to offer customers with culinary inspirations, it would be prudent to develop innovative and distinctive recipes that are not readily accessible online. Once they develop an affinity for your distinctive recipes, they will be inclined to engage with an advertisement on your website, potentially featuring a specific cream cheese brand or even baking trays. Additionally, it would be beneficial to explicitly acknowledge your utilization of these brands and provide hyperlinks in order to directly connect the products with the corresponding words. Your audience is guaranteed to engage with them!

Maintain the focus of the posts within the designated topic, while effectively instilling the notion in the reader's consciousness that acquisition of the promoted product or service is essential. You also have the option of including a contextual hyperlink to a specific product. Assist them in arriving at a conclusion, instead of attempting to immediately guide them to the sales website. The most effective strategy in this context is adopting a gentle approach, as it allows for a subtle promotion without being overt. I am certain that you have made numerous purchases through the act of clicking on advertisements displayed on the blogs and websites you frequent.

Enhance the Visibility of Your Website

Although it may seem self-evident, informing individuals about the existence of your website is imperative if you desire to attract visitors, ensure that your content is read, and encourage the utilization of your affiliate links. Regardless of whether it is a product or a service, it is imperative to engage in promotion in order to ensure widespread awareness of your offerings. Lacking adequate promotion, how do you intend to disseminate information about your website? There is a limited number of acquaintances who will choose to follow your links, and in order to secure a significant opportunity, you will require a minimum of 1000 clicks per week.

To begin with, it is recommended that you index your website in search engines, compose press releases for online distribution, and engage in active promotion of your site on forums relevant to your field of interest as well as social media platforms.

If you happen to have an acquaintance with a significantly influential blog, it could be worthwhile to approach them tactfully and inquire whether they would be open to discreetly endorsing yours on their platform. You may be required to contemplate remunerating them a nominal fee, as you will be deriving advantages from their provision of service. If you do not possess any acquaintances meeting this criterion, yet are aware of an individual who maintains a similar blog, you may contemplate reaching out to them tactfully to request their endorsement and promotion of yours. It is recommended to establish interconnected Facebook and Twitter accounts that are integrated with your website, ensuring that any updates made on the site are automatically shared on your social media platforms. Alternatively, it is possible to establish a Facebook page exclusively for your website or blog, through which you can consistently provide updates and direct links to your site. Focus on cultivating a loyal fan base, but refrain from resorting to purchasing followers. Purchasing followers will not result in genuine engagement on your website or clicks on the affiliate links. Instead, it merely creates a misleading perception of higher popularity for your social media account. You may have aspirations of attaining popularity, however, it is important to be mindful of the potential for great disappointment should these aspirations ultimately prove unfounded. If it happens to be a circle of acquaintances, ensure that they show genuine interest in your blog or website rather than simply doing you a favor. Such individuals have a tendency to remain in your life temporarily, but ultimately choose to withdraw when their interest wanes.

Please avoid being unnoticed or anonymous

This principle holds utmost significance. Primarily, it is imperative to possess unwavering self-assurance in one's identity and endeavors. Lacking self-assurance will be to your disadvantage. Merely because assuming an alias on the Internet offers facile concealment does not imply it is advisable to do so. It may be alluring to employ a trendy appellation, yet it is advised against. In order to establish credibility and generate income through online means, it is imperative to present oneself as an authentic individual, complete with accurate and verifiable contact information. Do refrain from concealing your identity with the use of a pseudonym or a username; instead, opt for divulging your true name and employ an email address linked to your personal domain, avoiding the usage of generic providers like Hotmail or AOL. If you desire to employ an alternative moniker, kindly contemplate denoting it within parentheses as a means to apprise the individual of your actual identity. Please ensure that you include your complete name, including initials, as there may exist multiple individuals sharing the same name as yours. It is imperative to maintain an open line of communication and assure individuals that they have the means to reach out with inquiries, with the guarantee of receiving a response from an actual human being. They may also request an authentic photograph for the purpose of positively verifying the identity of the individual in question. If there is a lack of trust in the Webmaster, individuals will be reluctant to click on the affiliate link, which will ultimately result in an absence of financial gain. It's all about trustworthiness.

Prior to commencing the monetization of affiliate marketing, it is imperative to ensure the establishment and optimization of your website to facilitate enhanced user engagement and incentivize them to actively click on the promotional hyperlinks. This entails the creation of high-quality content that is both informative and engaging, establishing oneself as a reputable authority in a specific field, and adopting a gentle approach towards promotional activities. Employ your expertise and passion to convincingly encourage the reader to proceed, rather than inundating the website with excessive advertising banners and shameless promotional tactics. Additionally, it is important to ensure that you furnish accurate contact information to establish your authenticity to your readers. Now that you have acquired the necessary readiness for selling, what are the most optimal affiliated products to engage with and what measures should you take to initiate the process?

The Originator And Trailblazer Of Affiliate Marketing

Michael is credited as the originator of affiliate marketing. He possesses an engineering degree, but discovered a strong affinity for the disciplines of marketing and sales. He founded his own enterprise known as ClickBank, an affiliate marketing platform dedicated to digital products.

Ted Nicholas is credited with being the individual who first introduced the concept of affiliate marketing. He devised this marketing strategy in the year 1996. Ted had perused a literary work titled How to Attain Success as an Affiliate, wherein the concept of leveraging third-party products or services within one's own online establishment to generate commissions from sales was expounded upon. Upon perusing the aforementioned literary work, he endeavored to devise an analogous approach tailored to his personal needs, leading to his exponential financial success within a span of two years.

CHAPTER SIX

Principles Governing Affiliate Marketing

The affiliate marketing sector is a lucrative industry worth billions of dollars. It boasts one of the highest conversion rates and is commonly hailed as one of the most profitable methods for generating leads and generating revenue on the internet.

Affiliate marketing provides marketers with a valuable mechanism to drive traffic and enhance sales of their products and services. Affiliate marketers are compensated for both product sales and the generation of potential customers. When an individual referred to your website subsequently becomes an affiliate, you have the opportunity to generate income on the basis of their subsequent actions, such as their engagement with any links present on your webpage.

The regulations pertaining to affiliate marketing comprise a collection of guidelines that dictate the conduct of both affiliates and merchants.

An essential principle of affiliate marketing is that affiliates are expected to consistently uphold ethical standards. They ought to refrain from engaging in spamming, establishing fraudulent websites, or pursuing illicit endeavors.

The second guideline entails that a representative should consistently utilize their individual website for the purpose of promoting products. This will assist individuals in establishing their reputation as a trustworthy seller, while also safeguarding the merchant from being perceived as a source of unsolicited communication within the marketplace.

The third guideline entails refraining from employing inaccurate or deceptive assertions while endorsing your links. This can result in a complete prohibition from engaging in an affiliate program and may also result in legal ramifications if your website promotes any inaccurate claims, irrespective of their relation to your link endeavor.

Chapter 13: Essential Prerequisites for Embarking on Affiliate Marketing

Below, I have outlined several significant subjects that are crucial for achieving expertise in the field of affiliate marketing and generating a substantial income from this highly lucrative online business. However, prior to delving into these essential topics, it is advisable to initially undertake the necessary foundational measures that will ensure a solid grasp on the fundamentals.

Chapter 14: The Promotional Channel in Affiliate Marketing

You have the ability to advertise and market any product across a multitude of social media platforms such as Google, Facebook, Twitter, Linkedin, and numerous others. What I consistently advocate and highly recommend is utilizing your personal blog for the purpose of affiliate marketing.

Engaging in product promotion through your personal blog will facilitate sustainable income generation over time. Furthermore, your blog offers the potential to augment your monetary gains through diverse avenues.

It would be advisable to familiarize oneself with additional methods, as previously indicated, such as leveraging and endorsing on social media platforms. However, it should be noted that the blog is the primary domain and should undoubtedly constitute an integral component of your promotional strategy.

Chapter 15: Selecting the Appropriate Product and Marketplace

I recommend that you select a product with which you have personal familiarity or that you frequently utilize in your everyday activities. The majority of products available in the online marketplace are affiliated with a corresponding link.

It encompasses a wide array of options, such as eBooks, web hosting services, website design themes, and numerous other possibilities. Ensure that you choose the optimal product that aligns with your specific niche.

If you are deficient in this aspect, you may experience a considerable influx of clicks, yet your conversion rates are likely to be nonexistent.

Presented herein, I offer a comprehensive compendium of invaluable advice to aid in the selection of commendable affiliate products for your esteemed blog or website.

Chapter 16: Developing a Persuasive Sales Presentation for a Wide Range of Products

In order to facilitate the sale of any product, it is necessary to craft a persuasive marketing message. The sales presentation may be presented as a blog post or can take the form of a dynamic or static webpage. Numerous enterprises offer a dedicated landing page for their products.

When crafting a sales presentation in straightforward language, it is imperative to ensure that your readers are fully informed about the value proposition and specific features attributed to the product or item they are considering for investment.

Before selecting your product, there are various factors that must be taken into consideration. Primarily, it is crucial to identify your specific target audience. Investigate whether you already possess an existing target audience that is relevant to the product in question, or if you must establish one from the beginning. If the latter is the case, it is imperative to develop a strategy to effectively engage and cater to this target audience through tailored content.

In either scenario, your approach will vary.

Chapter 17: Revealing Elusive Squeeze Page Techniques (Developing a Squeeze Page Without the Need for a Domain and Hosting)

A viable strategy for expanding your list of subscribers involves capturing leads via a squeeze landing page.

Generally, it is customary to possess a domain name and acquire web hosting for this purpose. However, in accordance with the aforementioned title of this book, I shall demonstrate an alternate method by which you can effortlessly generate a squeeze landing page devoid of a traditional website.

Indeed, there is no requirement for domain acquisition or hosting whatsoever. I have imparted this technique to my students, as it entails simplicity and cost-effectiveness. Curiously, it remains somewhat underutilized in the broader public.

Could you please provide a detailed explanation of what a squeeze landing page entails?

The landing page has a straightforward design aimed at prompting visitors to subscribe to your mailing list, enabling you to acquire their contact details and subsequently engage with them.

Chapter 18: Concealing Links in Affiliate Marketing

One of the primary apprehensions associated with Affiliate marketing pertains to the optimization of search engine rankings. The majority of affiliate marketers overlook the importance of adequately optimizing their blogs to ensure their blogs are search engine optimization (SEO) compliant.

During the subsequent lesson, I elucidated the manner in which search engines, notably Google, handle affiliate links and the practice of disguising them to appear pertinent and user-centric.

Strategies for Enhancing Sales and Maximizing Profit through Marketing

It will become increasingly apparent that the maxim "continuously engage in promotion" is highly applicable to you, especially considering your role as an affiliate marketer. It is imperative to disseminate information regarding the solutions you are advocating for, as well as actively champion and endorse them. Only at that point will the information be disseminated. There are diverse methods available for promoting your affiliate business that necessitate minimal financial investment, if any at all, and instead rely on the commitment of your time.

Please bear in mind that your organization may have multiple aspects that require promotion. It will be your duty to promote your affiliate program to individuals who demonstrate an interest in generating income from it. You are required to identify individuals or groups who possess a demand for the products you create or acquire, and consequently promote and sell those products to them. As a result of this, it presents a situation involving interactions between businesses and consumers, necessitating the adoption of distinct sales approaches for each.

You have the option to market either one by employing the same approach, however, the manner in which you present the content will vary based on the characteristics of your target audience and the inherent attributes of the product being promoted. Content marketing ought to be regarded as the primary marketing strategy for your company.

Marketing with Content

This classification of marketing encompasses various forms of content-driven marketing, including marketing via social media platforms, email campaigns, and blogging. Devise a comprehensive strategic plan for each individual product that you anticipate offering in the future. Prior to commencing production, ascertain the intended target audience, intended display platform, and the desired directive in order to adequately generate the material.

Enhancing Search Engine Performance

It is imperative for your success that you acquire extensive knowledge regarding SEO. With the aid of this resource, you will enhance your ability to produce superior headlines, subject lines, and overall content that is effectively tailored to the intended audience. It is of utmost significance to bear in mind that search engine optimization (SEO) encompasses a combination of on-page and off-page strategies. Some of these encompass the establishment of intra-document references in addition to the procurement of external associations to your content. The incorporation of software, such as Yoast SEO, into your blog may prove to be highly advantageous.

Paid Marketing

Highly accomplished affiliate marketers employ paid advertising strategies in conjunction with the complimentary avenues at their disposal. Please be aware that you do not possess true autonomy in this matter. You will be solely responsible for bearing the costs, be it in terms of either time or financial resources. The path you select is contingent upon both the capacities you possess and the priorities you hold in your life.

Methods for Determining Market Demand

Market demand analysis refers to the evaluation of the demand for a product and the determination of the potential marketability and saleability of the product within the existing market.

It considers the product's availability through other competing companies, as well as the subsequent competition that arises from introducing our own product into the market.

Gaining insight into the market demand is a crucial factor in assessing product profitability and attaining the revenue objectives of both the company and the particular product as a cost center.

Various procedures and techniques are employed to assess market demand, and among a few, the following factors are discussed -.

How to ascertain the target demographic?

The initial measure to assess product demand entails identifying the target market. The target market may consist of a subset within a larger market or encompass the entirety of the market, contingent upon the nature of the product being offered.

For instance, let us consider the scenario where you are engaged in the sale of pickup trucks. As a salesperson, it is imperative to comprehend the unique selling proposition (USP) of a pickup truck and ascertain the customary demographic profile of its customers. An individual attired in formal attire entering the premises does not inevitably signify a potential consumer seeking to purchase a pickup truck.

He could potentially be in search of either a hatchback or a sedan, given the information available. Attempting to convince him to consider purchasing a pickup truck is highly likely to result in him becoming disinterested, ultimately leading to a permanent loss of his attention. Gaining insight into your target demographic and its unique needs is the initial phase in developing an effective marketing strategy and achieving profitability for your business.

How to Gain Insight into Market Competition

Gaining comprehensive knowledge about the market competition and the market share held by various customers is a crucial endeavor when seeking to comprehend market demand. The analysis of the current products and their unique selling propositions (USPs), along with a comparative evaluation of your products and those offered by your competitors, are fundamental components required to initiate a comprehensive market demand analysis.

How can one gain insights into customer behavior?

It is noteworthy to mention that one must possess the capacity to comprehend consumer behavior and the patterns underlying decision-making. An intriguing occurrence will serve to elucidate the matter further. A few years ago, we made the decision to upgrade our outdated refrigerator and proceeded to visit an electronics store to evaluate the selection of models available. It was somewhat tardy, and it appeared that the proprietor was likely nearing the designated time for closure.

We were in the process of evaluating and selecting the final model among a range of 4-5 options. As we were approaching the concluding decision, I glanced at the proprietor of the shop and observed his apprehensive gaze fixated on his timepiece, accompanied by a noticeable manifestation of irritation on his countenance.

I became aware of this fact and promptly conveyed my apologies to him for causing a delay beyond what was originally intended. Rather than politely accepting it and asking me to continue, he responded by acknowledging that we were indeed detaining him and pointing out that it was about to close.

Slightly astonished, I chose to defer my decision and once again apologized as I exited the store. A skilled salesperson would endeavor to comprehend and anticipate the thoughts and desires of the customer. It was evident in our behavior that my wife and I were not simply browsing, but actively deliberating on which one to purchase, as we inadvertently displayed ample indications of our intentions. However, he elected to disregard those indications and adopt a straightforward approach. Approximately three days later, we did indeed purchase the new refrigerator; however, we opted not to revisit that particular store.

Methods for comprehending the product lifecycle or the developmental phase in which the product is currently positioned within the market

This holds significant importance as you wouldn't want to enter a market that is already saturated in terms of demand. At any given point in time, the market may exhibit the following stages of demand –

(a) Greater demand than supply. This is commonly marked by an initial phase wherein there is an elevated level of product demand exceeding the available supply.

In this phase, it can be observed that the demand is at its maximum and both the supply and demand are in a state of equilibrium. This concept may also be referred to as the point of equilibrium. Given the high level of demand and supply, the market is typically saturated with competitors who are all endeavoring to promote and sell their products through various advertising and promotional methods.

(c) The final stage is characterized by a decline in demand for the product. The frequency of launches for newer products is relatively low and the profit margins are significantly diminished due to prevailing competition, as well as an excess supply compared to demand. This represents the final phase of the product life cycle prior to its discontinuation and removal from production.

We can provide illustrations of television here to underscore the point. CRT television sets were predominant during the initial stages of television development.

While there is still some demand and sales in certain markets, it has been completely phased out of circulation in the majority of countries. Stores are no longer stocking these items and there is virtually no demand for them anymore. The latest advancements in television technology, such as LCD, LED, 3D, and Smart TV systems, are the sole options sought after by consumers. Currently, these objects are in different phases of the early stages of their life cycle, whereas CRT televisions are in the final stage of the same cycle.

How can one develop a unique selling proposition for their products?

How do your products distinguish themselves from the other varieties currently available in the market? May I inquire about the specific market segment your products are intended to cater to and serve as a unique selling proposition (USP) for your sales team?

After conducting extensive market research and thoroughly understanding the consumer demand for the product, it becomes imperative to establish a profitable blog and generate a substantial amount of traffic to the said blog. This not only enhances your reputation, but also generates sales effortlessly and autonomously.

In order to gain a comprehensive understanding of this particular aspect, let us now transition to the subsequent phase outlined in this guide.

How to Establish a Lucrative WordPress Blog

Welcome to Stage 3 of this guide. At this juncture, it is imperative to transition towards practical implementation, as you have successfully employed the strategies outlined in Stage 2 in order to identify a lucrative product with minimal competition and significant market demand.

For the sake of further simplification, it is advisable for beginners to opt for a product with a gravity range of 10-50.

By following this approach, one can efficiently locate a product within a relatively short time frame and subsequently implement the various strategies provided in Stage 2 in a gradual manner.

Now that we have acquired our product, it is imperative that we proceed with the establishment of our wordpress website.

In this phase, we will acquire an understanding of the implementation process for setting up our website, and subsequently proceed to generate traffic to our platform.

Without further delay, let us proceed expeditiously towards the development of our inaugural lucrative website.

Establishing A Customer Base And Promoting Your Merchandise

In terms of achieving success in the sale of affiliate products, the initial measure towards accomplishing this is to build a target audience. This presents the central condition, if there may be any, as it suggests that it will be necessary for one to personally invest a significant amount of time and exertion to maximize sales potential. Nevertheless, by doing so, you will maximize your earning potential.

A positive aspect is that by choosing a subject that arouses your curiosity, you will essentially have the opportunity to generate substantial earnings while indulging in an activity that provides you with enjoyment.

However, prior to attaining this position, it is imperative to first cultivate an audience and establish credibility as a respected figure within the community.

Existmorechannelsthroughwhichaffiliate productscanbesold? Certainly! Furthermore, we shall explore those subjects within this specific chapter. However, it is crucial to emphasize the significance of nurturing an audience and ensuring their engagement with your business.

Strategies for Creating a Marketable Brand

Attaining such a degree of influence is not devoid of its own set of difficulties. In order to attain the stage wherein individuals make purchases solely based on your endorsement, it will be necessary to allocate a substantial amount of time and exert sincere endeavor to consistently provide authentic and valuable contributions over an extended duration.

Commencing the process involves the creation of a website and establishing a dynamic presence across diverse social media channels. Rather than rushing to make a sale, it is advisable to allocate time to cultivate trust and loyalty among prospective customers. This can be achieved by consistently providing valuable content as an integral part of a sustained marketing endeavor.

Which of these options holds the highest degree of importance? Develop a brand that exhibits a noticeable and influential identity, accompanied by a compelling declaration of purpose and a clearly outlined representation of the target audience. The customer persona serves as an imaginative portrayal of the most desirable clientele for your organization. Making an endeavor to create a website that possesses comprehensive relevance and utmost appeal within the limits of human possibility constitutes a grave error. This methodology could be considered flawed due to the identical reason underlying the initial flaws observed in the digital goods you purchased. The underlying cause of this phenomenon is that to cultivate a lackluster and unappealing brand image, one must necessarily pursue a wide-ranging approach, thus accounting for this state of affairs.

For instance, a website dedicated to the theme of "fitness" is overly expansive and excessively inundated with content, rendering it improbable to achieve success. This implies facing competition from the vast majority of the online realm. What strategies do you employ to set yourself apart in a highly competitive market?

Consider the development of a website centered around fitness targeting individuals above the age of 40, instead. Alternatively, why not consider an option known as Paleo Fitness? Also, CrossFit. Or Outdoor Fitness. Alternatively, Extreme Bodybuilding.

Each of these alternatives possesses a markedly more distinct target audience, a considerably more specific goal statement, and a more captivating hook. Each of them will cater to a more limited audience, however, this specific audience will have a significantly higher probability of engaging and finding satisfaction in the existence of a tailored offering that precisely addresses their requirements.

Following the establishment of this unequivocal and passionate objective, the brand should subsequently emerge. This implies that upon observing your company logo or the design aesthetic of your website, individuals ought to promptly discern whether or not it will be aesthetically appealing to them. Your organization ought to possess a distinct means of effectively communicating its target audience and core values, while ensuring that the generated content aligns with these assertions.

The anticipated aesthetic of the hardcore bodybuilding website entails a red and black color palette, wherein a significant quantity of somber photographs showcasing extraordinarily muscular individuals will be showcased, alongside articles discussing the augmentation of testosterone through compound lifts.

In contrast, it is likely that the paleo fitness website will feature a color palette consisting of green and white, accompanied by imagery depicting individuals engaging in outdoor jogging amidst the invigorating ambiance of nature. The entirety of one's surroundings is visible from this location.

All aspects of your brand, encompassing your advertising, social media presence, and all other forms of content, should maintain congruence with this established image.

The selection of the affiliate product that aligns with your business requirements should also factor in the target demographic. Furthermore, it is imperative that you promote it in this manner, and the success of sales will rely on this unique selling proposition. Equally significant, the content you present should exhibit freshness and authenticity, demonstrating your genuine expertise in the field.

Engaging a writer who lacks knowledge in the subject matter you have hired them to write about will severely impede your chances of achieving success in selling the affiliate product. Why?

Due to the writer being paid solely for conducting research and paraphrasing the information using their own language abilities.

This implies that all of the material will lack originality and depth, and it also suggests the potential for it to be outdated or incorrect (considering that the individuals may lack sufficient knowledge about the subject to discern such circumstances).

You have two options: either you should personally undertake the task of writing it or seek out a writer who possesses genuine enthusiasm for the subject matter. Why? As this occurs, individuals will acquire novel and intriguing perspectives. For there is a perpetual quest for fresh insights among people, it is through this means that one can effectively position themselves as a leading intellectual, captivating the attention of others and garnering their interest in both engaging with your discourse and subscribing to your newsletter.

Be bold. Be distinctive. Be passionate. The subsequent action entails choosing a product that effectively caters to the identical target audience. Is it that there is an insufficient amount of time available for such a task? There is no cause for alarm; additional options, which are elaborated upon subsequently, are also at your disposal.

Successfully Establishing Link Placement
Being an affiliate marketer, the process of selling becomes exceedingly effortless. You will be furnished with a single hyperlink, exclusively designated for promoting a product. Upon strategically embedding this hyperlink, you will become eligible to generate sales and subsequently accrue earnings from the resulting purchases.

The current inquiry pertains to the precise location in which you intend to place it.

Most of us are likely to choose a landing page or sales page as the preferred option for placing our link, however, it is important to note that this is just one among several potential alternatives. In this section, we will explore the functionalities of that system, alongside a range of alternative options that are currently accessible.

Creating a Marketing Page

A webpage that has been specifically designed with the primary purpose of promoting and vending a product or service is commonly known as a sales page on a website. This implies that it will not furnish any additional material, such as articles, and is unlikely to offer any supplementary links or advertisements as well. It is imperative to avoid any elements in this vicinity that may serve as distractions from the products or services being presented.

Typically, a sales page is designed to be elongated and slender, thereby compelling visitors to engage in continuous scrolling and hence dedicating more time to thoroughly peruse the content you wish to convey. As a result of this, their departure without making a purchase would be significantly hindered, given that they would harbor the sentiment of having squandered their time.

Nevertheless, writing holds paramount importance. If you possess the ability to craft a compelling sales pitch, you will have the opportunity to capitalize on this captive audience and convert them into enthusiastic purchasers.

The power of persuasive writing is a formidable tool that possesses the potential to elevate one's prowess as a marketing virtuoso. These are not the drones for which you have been seeking...

Having adept skills in employing persuasive language can greatly enhance your efficacy in sales, acquiring subscribers for your list, and ultimately accomplishing any desired objective. Ultimately, possessing the skill to effectively employ language as a means of influencing an audience equates to possessing the ability to employ language as a means of influencing an audience.

So, how exactly does one go about acquiring such a superpower? The subsequent recommendations will prove to be valuable...

Efficiently capture individuals' attention since many individuals are pressed for time and prefer concise content. To effectively persuade the individuals in your audience, the initial measure entails enticing them to peruse the content you present. What is your approach to accomplishing that? One possible method is to initiate with a declarative statement that carries strong emphasis.

An additional method of capturing individuals' attention is to utilize a narrative framework. The latter approach proves to be notably efficacious as it diverges from our inherent inclination to disengage from a narrative prior to discovering its ultimate resolution.

• Present a compelling case using evidence and statistics: Individuals may exhibit hesitancy in accepting your assertions since they lack personal knowledge of you and are aware of your sales motive. Nevertheless, by leveraging factual information and numerical data, you have the potential to earn their confidence. Alternatively, it is advisable to let the data speak for itself. The greater the quantity of factual data and numerical evidence you are able to reference, along with the incorporation of highly respected sources to bolster your stance, the more persuasive your argument will become.

• Foresee: It is imperative to make every effort to foresee the concerns that your readers may have and to promptly address those issues. One could potentially highlight the abundance of impressive options available on the internet, but subsequently underscore that this particular endeavor distinguishes itself as far more than a mere fraudulent scheme.

• Decrease the probability of unfavorable results by leveraging individuals' inherent aversion to loss, suggesting that they are more inclined to preserve their present possessions rather than pursue new acquisitions. In the event that this scenario arises, it is imperative to mitigate any potential risks by offering customers the assurance of money-back guarantees and complimentary trial periods. Primarily, it is crucial to understand the value proposition. The emotional value of your product is reflected in the manner in which you assure that its purchase will profoundly affect the lives of your audience members. As an example, in the case of marketing an eBook on fitness, it is essential to ensure that your promotional message effectively communicates that the product being offered extends beyond a mere eBook on fitness.

The concept of possessing boundless energy, well-defined abdominal muscles, and abundant self-assurance is undeniably the core of your offering, thus ensuring its effective promotion is imperative. It is imperative that you stay focused on this aspect! Appeal to the recipient's emotions and strive to stimulate a reaction from them, preferably evoking a sense of enthusiasm towards acquiring your product.

It is important to note that most digital products are typically accompanied by pre-made sales pages, such as the one provided, allowing for easy incorporation by simply copying and pasting the entire script onto your own website.

Given that you already possess a sales page, the only remaining task to initiate conversions entails guiding your target audience towards said page. This objective can be achieved by leveraging the utilization of emails, alongside the proactive marketing of your products on your diverse array of social media channels. You also have the option to display advertisements for the product in the sidebar of your website or in other designated areas on your site.

Establishing a Retail Establishment

If you have a diverse range of affiliate products for sale, which can be considered a strategically advantageous business decision, it may be advisable to establish a dedicated store for their sale. This suggests that you will be emphasizing and promoting items that align with your brand, akin to the way you would in an online shop. The sole notable alteration pertains to the redirection of buyers, who, upon clicking on your item, will no longer be directed to your webpage, but instead, will be redirected to an entirely distinct website.

This task can be easily accomplished, exemplified by utilizing the WooCommerce e-commerce plugin, known for its seamless integration with the WordPress platform. This feature will afford you the opportunity to establish an online retail platform integrated within your website, providing customers with the ability to peruse merchandise and complete transactions. It possesses compatibility with affiliate content, thereby ensuring that any time an individual clicks on an item, they will be seamlessly redirected to a distinct webpage that incorporates your referral link.

Additional points of market entry

Nevertheless, have you taken into consideration the possibility of integrating hyperlinks throughout the body of your articles? Despite the limited utilization of this function by affiliates, the act of capitalizing on a website or blog through advertising presents an excellent prospect. You simply need to compose content pertaining to the subject matter that you possess a keen interest in discussing, and subsequently incorporate a hyperlink to your affiliate program within the piece. By adopting this approach, you will have the opportunity to discreetly promote the product, resulting in a higher likelihood of attracting individuals who are genuinely interested in your content and consequently more inclined to click on it. Similar to the integration of AdSense on your webpage, with the distinction being that you would obtain a significantly higher commission and have the ability to actively encourage individuals to click on the provided link. You are even permitted to openly acknowledge that it generates financial profits!

Indeed, it is a legal obligation in numerous jurisdictions around the globe for individuals to make it known that they are not deriving any financial gain from the transaction of those items. One can effortlessly achieve this by employing a plugin that inserts a message at the footer of every page on your website; however, it is imperative not to overlook this task.

The compilation of the foremost ten items represents an exceptionally efficacious mode of content, specifically intended to promote affiliate products. If you operate within the fitness industry, you have the opportunity to construct a comprehensive compilation highlighting the top-rated domestic workout equipment. Similarly, if you specialize in technology writing, you can compose an informative piece devoted to exploring the latest cutting-edge laptops currently accessible in the market.

Regardless of the course of action you choose, this strategy presents a remarkable opportunity for generating a substantial number of web visits and revenue. Additionally, it holds significant potential for leveraging rich snippets, thereby significantly enhancing your search result rankings.

Enhance the visibility of your content in the search engine results pages (SERPs).

Similarly, there are no obstacles or limitations prohibiting you from including a hyperlink to your affiliate program within the primary content of an email communication. This approach serves as an exceptional means of reaching out to individuals directly through their email inbox, precisely when they are most likely to be responsive to the offers or opportunities you wish to present.

Furthermore, it is feasible to incorporate affiliate links within ebooks. If you are engaged in the sale of digital products or wish to offer a complimentary download, you possess the capability to incorporate hyperlinks within your PDF document. It is highly likely that individuals perusing this content have already displayed a considerable level of interest in your enterprise, thus increasing the likelihood of their patronage towards the products you endorse. These leads possess the necessary qualifications, rendering this environment highly suitable for attempting to sell items of even greater value.

Envision the possibility of effortlessly generating revenue by selling a digital product at a price point of $20 per item, and subsequently accumulating a substantial sum through the multitude of individuals who engage with your book and diligently implement the prescribed suggestions.

An alternative course of action could involve incorporating a hyperlink to your affiliate program within a tangible promotional document such as a pamphlet or booklet. The optimal approach to implementing this technique involves initially generating a URL that is easily recollected and uncomplicated, and subsequently redirecting that particular URL to your affiliate link. Through utilizing this method, you will have the opportunity to directly promote your products to prospective clientele.

One need not consistently engage in active product promotion; an alternative approach could be the use of a subtle sales technique by incorporating the link, possibly accompanied by an image. That's part of the aim of these suggestions; to demonstrate that you don't always have to be actively marketing the product.

This particularly exhibits noteworthy efficacy when employed for tangible entities, particularly when employing an impeccably crafted button that is directly associated with the content present on the webpage. If you possess an exceptionally thriving website with a substantial number of visitors and a vast amount of content, one effective strategy would be to strategically integrate purchase links throughout the site in the aforementioned manner. This approach would likely result in a gradual influx of sales, ultimately culminating in a significant accumulation thereof.

With the application of creative thinking, affiliate links can be implemented in a multitude of diverse circumstances. Engage in experimentation and exploration of diverse methodologies; you may encounter unexpected results as to which strategy proves to be the most effective for both you and your product.

Supplementing Marketing Strategies with PPC Advertising

However, in the event that there is an absence of individuals available to attentively hear your words, what course of action should be pursued? What would be the result or how would it affect your audience in the event that they do +

Do you not perceive yourself as a respected and trustworthy authority in their eyes? Inthisscenario,youwillneedtodevelopstrategiestoredirectpeopledirectly

tothepagewhereyouaresellingyourproductorservice. Thegoodnewsisthat

This task can be accomplished with relative ease by employing the use of PPC (pay-per-click).

Social media platforms such as Facebook and online advertising channels like AdWords.

In the context of pay-per-click (PPC) advertising, you will incur charges solely based on the instances where a user takes action and clicks on your ad.

engages with your advertisement through a click. You have the authority to establish the upper limit.

desired expenditure per click" and "threshold at which

Your allotted budget will be fully depleted. If you have incurred expenditure in terms of cost-per-click (CPC)

If the bid is placed at a low value, the advertisement may not be displayed on the results page.

Numerous advertisements from competing firms are being directed towards the same specific market segment. If you

If the value is established at an excessively elevated level, there exists a significant likelihood that a profit will not be generated. When utilizing Facebook as a platform for advertising, you will be granted the capability to
Select the target audience for displaying the advertisements based on
The data provided by users through the social networking platform. These are the
ones:
- Age
- Gender
- Location
- Personal pastimes and areas of interest
- Job title
- Income bracket
- The welfare of others • The concerns of others • The preferences of others • The needs of others • The priorities of others

When engaging in advertising on Google via the AdWords platform, it is crucial to consider not only the individual's interests (as inferred from their search queries, often referred to as "keywords"), but also their underlying intent.

When considering pay-per-click marketing, one must give due consideration to intent as it serves as a pivotal determinant, indicating whether an individual is merely conducting informational research or genuinely seeking to engage in a purchase.

Should they be engaged in the pursuit of research, it is plausible for them to seek out information on the "best computer games of the current year." Moreover, if potential buyers express an inclination to make a purchase, they might initiate an online search using either the precise title of the game or the phrase "affordable computer games." Additionally, the utilization of "negative keywords" holds relevance, as it allows for the exclusion of phrases that may insinuate a lack of interest in purchasing, thereby indicating an inappropriate intention - such as the phrase "free download."

PPC has been strategically developed to cater to individuals who are more inclined to make a purchase, encouraging them to click on the link. This objective aligns with the overarching strategy. This serves to reduce the overall investment amount required while simultaneously increasing the potential reward. This implies that the advertisements must be precisely tailored to reach the intended audience, going as far as excluding individuals who are unlikely to be interested in making a purchase by carefully selecting the appropriate content.

As a matter of course, for the purpose of maximizing your earnings, it is essential that the hyperlink directs users to a webpage where they are able to complete a transaction. Subsequently, it is imperative to direct your attention towards the degree of conversion achieved by your website. In alternative terms, if your landing page exhibits well-crafted content, it has the potential to achieve a conversion rate of 1%, suggesting that approximately 1% of visitors would engage in a transaction or purchase from your offering. By augmenting this quantity, you will acquire a larger sum of funds that can be allocated towards advertising, all the while upholding your present degree of profitability.

Leveraging the Potential of Facebook and Alternative Platforms for Direct Sales

Evidently, an additional option available to you would be to directly vend your merchandise through one of those alternative avenues. There are no impediments to including a link to one of your affiliated products on your Facebook group page or Instagram account, either in your biography section or once the swipe up feature becomes available for adding to your stories. If you lack the requisite knowledge or availability to establish a website, this is a beneficial alternative for cultivating an actively engaged audience for your content.

Leveraging the "Camtasia" Video Software to Drive Increased Traffic and User Engagement

With the increasing number of individuals partaking in affiliate marketing, it is unsurprising that the intensity of competition has escalated. The objective is to discover a means of surpassing fellow collaborators. Furthermore, this affiliate will acquire valuable insights and techniques to meticulously devise a superior strategy that will enhance the program's functionality and generate increased revenue.

How could one possibly make a stronger impact on their audience and clientele than by capturing and distributing high-quality, immersive video content? There is no greater satisfaction than witnessing the dissemination of your diligent efforts, arousing anticipation among customers to procure your product on the spot. Camtasia in action. This is an established and substantiated fact. The provision of tangible items to customers has the potential to rapidly trigger a significant upsurge in online sales. No prior training or educational background is necessary for comprehending the functioning of this system within your affiliate program. Individuals of all backgrounds possess the capability to produce exceptional videos through the utilization of informative multimedia tutorials and comprehensive presentations that can be accessed via the internet. The procedure resembles the presence of a client beside you, observing your desk, and visually and verbally conveying their specific desires. This entire process was carried out in a sequential manner.

Can someone kindly provide a detailed explanation of the functioning of Camtasia for those who are unfamiliar? Capture desktop operations effortlessly with a single click. There is no necessity to preserve and compile all the files as they will be incorporated at a subsequent time. It is a straightforward task to transform the video into a webpage. Following the conversion, it will be possible for you to provide your customers with access to that particular page. Videos offer enhanced comprehensibility and assimilation compared to textual material, the consumption of which frequently poses challenges. Please load your page. Distribute content through weblog platforms, Really Simple Syndication feeds, and audio broadcasts. Expanding the global distribution of your camtasia videos can enable them to reach a wider audience and attract potential customers in various regions. There is no greater advantage than being showcased across numerous websites and platforms in order to enhance personal promotion and effectively convey one's message.

The affiliate program offered by Camtasia facilitates various functionalities. You may...

Utilize your complete sensory faculties to craft exquisite multimedia presentations that have been demonstrated to amplify sales. Additionally, it alleviates any uncertainties among dissatisfied customers. Minimize returns and additional customer concerns through the provision of a visual presentation illustrating the proper usage and correct handling of the product. The incidence of complaints is likewise diminished as the customer has the opportunity to witness and perceive all pertinent information and demonstrations.

Utilize visual presentations to effectively advertise and endorse affiliate products and services. This strategy serves as an efficient method for redirecting viewers to your affiliate site following the conclusion of the video. In conclusion, optimize your presentation by emphasizing the specific site location and requesting that individuals visit said location directly for further details.

Enhance your online auction presence by providing your readers with a comprehensive overview of your offerings, thereby maximizing your potential results. A photo auction is projected to yield a significant fourfold increase in the auction rate. Consider the potential magnitude that would emanate from possessing a video. Publish substantial informational products that can be marketed at significantly elevated prices. It is highly valuable given its vibrant graphical interface and extensive range of templates.

Enhance customer satisfaction through error reduction. Initially, promptly showcasing your desired objectives effectively illustrates the inherent worth of an affiliate program. One can appreciate the advantage of multimedia in that errors and malfunctions are a rare occurrence. It's already here. These are merely a few of the capabilities that Camtasia offers, which can prove highly advantageous in your selected affiliate program.

The primary objective of utilizing Camtasia is to enhance the revenue generated through your affiliate program. Its application for entertainment and amusement notwithstanding, such trivial motives do not justify a serious pursuit of the subject.

Direct your attention towards your objectives and attain them through strategic actions that are conducive to enhancing your earning potential.

Boost Commissions Overnight

The captivating realm of affiliate marketing does not encompass website acquisition, customer transactions, cash back, product development, and maintenance. This method presents itself as a straightforward approach to initiating an online business venture and enhancing one's financial gains. If it is presumed that you are engaged in an affiliate program, what course of action would you pursue thereafter? Obtain a commission that is twice or thrice the standard rate. Correct? What is the appropriate course of action to take in this situation? Presented below are potent strategies to expeditiously elevate the fees associated with your affiliate program. Uncover the most exceptional advertising software and products.

Clearly, your objective is to endorse a program that maximizes profitability within a condensed timeframe. There are multiple aspects that warrant consideration when selecting such a program. Select an option that offers a favorable fee structure. Provide merchandise that caters to the needs of your intended demographic. It has consistently demonstrated a successful track record of promptly and effortlessly compensating affiliates. If you are unable to augment your investment, I recommend discontinuing your participation in this program and seeking out an alternative that better aligns with your goals and resources.

There is a multitude of affiliate programs available on the Internet that provide compelling justifications for selection. It is advisable to opt for the most effective advertisements in order to avoid wastage of advertising expenses. Generate complimentary reports or concise e-books to disseminate on your website. There is a higher probability of engaging in competition with fellow partners who are promoting the same program.

One can establish a distinctive identity among fellow affiliates by initially crafting a concise report on the products being promoted. We offer complimentary reports containing valuable insights. If feasible, include suggestions for recommended products. E-books give you confidence. Your clientele will perceive this display from your end and be enticed to sample the offerings you provide. We gather and retain the email addresses of individuals who access complimentary e-Books. It is widely recognized that individuals do not make purchases on a whim. It may be advantageous to transmit multiple messages exceeding a quantity of six in order to promote the sale of a product or service. This is the fundamental rationale behind our practice of gathering the contact details of individuals who download reports and e-books. You have the ability to monitor the progress of this contact and gently reiterate the importance of making a purchase.

Obtain the contact details of the prospect prior to submitting them on the vendor's website. Please be advised that we provide complimentary advertising services to individuals who own products. The act of generating income solely occurs through the process of selling. If a prospective customer is directed straight to a supplier, it is possible to permanently forfeit their business. Upon acquiring knowledge of their identities, you can subsequently transmit additional marketing communications aimed at securing recurring commissions as opposed to one-time transactions. Publish an online newsletter. It is more advisable to offer a product suggestion to an acquaintance, as opposed to selling it to an unfamiliar individual. The objective behind the creation of your own newsletter is to serve this purpose.

Additionally, you can cultivate trustworthy relationships with the individuals subscribing to your services. This approach effectively maintains a nuanced equilibrium between imparting meaningful information and promoting sales. Through the perpetuation of informative opinion pieces, you can foster a climate of shared comprehension among your audience, thereby motivating their endorsement and subsequent acquisition of your product. Benefit from augmented commission rates offered by sellers.

Should you have already achieved success in a specific campaign, it will be necessary for you to liaise with the seller in order to establish mutual agreement concerning the allocation of a percentage for the sales commission. If the merchant exhibits astuteness, they can satisfy your request without incurring any loss of valued merchandise. Keep in mind that you represent a safe and secure investment option for your traders. Do not hesitate to enroll for commission. Be reasonable about it. Write powerful pay-per-click ads. Search Engine Pay-Per-Click (PPC) advertising represents the optimal approach to effectively promote products and services on the internet. Associates have the opportunity to generate a modest revenue by overseeing pay-per-click (PPC) campaigns such as those offered by Google AdWords and Overture. Next, evaluate its effectiveness to determine the most optimal approaches and identify those that ought to be eliminated.

Implement these strategies and witness an immediate impact on your commission earnings.

Avoiding Common Errors in Affiliate Marketing

Given that the guide is nearing its final stages of completion and the publication is on the verge of being finalized, allow me to present a comprehensive overview of warning indicators and treacherous territories that should be circumvented when delving into the realm of affiliate marketing.

So listen...
Affiliate marketing is widely recognized as an exceedingly efficient and influential method for generating income on the internet. This program offers the opportunity for individuals to generate income through online means. Since these affiliate marketing programs are easy to follow, follow and pay regular commissions, more people are now willing to engage in this business.

Nevertheless, akin to any enterprise, affiliate marketing ventures encounter numerous challenges. Committing several prevalent errors can result in a significant reduction of marketers' daily profits. Hence, it is advisable to refrain from engaging in it to prevent subsequent remorse.

Error number one: Selecting an unsuitable partner.

The majority of individuals endeavor to achieve rapid financial gains through the means of affiliate marketing. They have a propensity for selecting simplistic products due to their desire to be associated with them. These are the product categories that the program deems as being "trending". They opt for products where there is significant demand, without considering their personal affinity towards the product. This decision is certainly unwise. Select the products of utmost significance to you, rather than those deemed superior. In order for any undertaking to achieve success, it is imperative to allocate sufficient time towards strategic planning and meticulous delineation of actions. Choose your favorite product. Subsequently, conduct thorough investigations on the aforementioned product to ascertain its market demand. It is comparatively simpler to market a product that holds personal sentiment compared to marketing a product purely for financial gain.

Error #2: Enroll in an excessive number of affiliate programs. We highly encourage the endeavor of participating in multiple affiliate programs in order to optimize your income, considering that they present a straightforward registration process. Moreover, one could hold the perception that there is no inherent issue with participating in numerous affiliate programs and that there is no potential detriment to be incurred. Indeed, diversifying one's income streams is a highly advantageous approach. Nevertheless, attempting to simultaneously manipulate multiple applications while logged in would result in an inability to effectively concentrate on each individual one. result? The affiliate program will not achieve its full potential and the resulting revenue will fall short of the initial expectations. The most effective approach to attain favorable outcomes is to enroll in a program that offers a commission rate that is at least 40%. Subsequently, exert full effort by fervently promoting your product. After confirming a satisfactory level of profitability, you may proceed to enroll in an additional affiliate program.

The strategy lies in gradually and undoubtedly accomplishing the task. There is no need to hurry, particularly when it pertains to affiliate marketing. Based on current trends, it appears that the future holds great promise and it is expected that affiliate marketing will continue to thrive for a prolonged period. Error #3: Failing to procure a product or avail oneself of a service.

As an affiliate, your primary objective entails efficiently and consistently promoting your product or service while identifying prospective clientele. In order to attain this objective, it is imperative that you possess the capability to provide said products and services to your clientele. So it proves to be challenging if one does not attempt it personally.

Try these. Consequently, I am unable to confidently endorse it. Additionally, it would be undesirable for your clients to utilize the products/services provided by your company. Prior to enrolling as an affiliate, it is prudent to assess the efficacy of your product or service, ensuring it meets the promised standards. If such an individual exists, they would most likely be characterized as a loyal and self-aware individual with a strong sense of their own capabilities and limitations. Subsequently, your clientele will perceive a profound sense of authenticity and sincerity from you, thereby motivating them to embark on their own experiential journey.

Numerous affiliate marketers commit this error and expend excessive funds on their efforts. Make every effort possible to prevent these mistakes. By doing so, you can avoid finding yourself in this particular predicament.

Time is the key. Allocate sufficient time to conduct a thorough assessment of your marketing strategy to ensure its alignment with your objectives. With proper execution, one can optimize their affiliate marketing program to achieve substantial profits.

With this, you are well-prepared to commence. Affiliate marketing is a lucrative source of income in the present era, and you have been provided with a comprehensive analysis of the dos and don'ts in this regard. After the implementation, you may peruse alternative literature as a means of acquiring financial guidance.

- "Strategies for generating wealth through intelligent financial approaches"
- "Effective methods for achieving significant financial gains"
- "Insights on prudent tactics for accumulating substantial wealth"
- "Practical approaches to attaining financial success through smart and ethical means"
- "Techniques for prospering financially through intelligent and strategic actions"

www.ingramcontent.com/pod-product-compliance
Lightning Source LLC
Chambersburg PA
CBHW050251120526
44590CB00016B/2306